NAME:_____

MW01131456

Date:_____

We want to see you THRIVE and experience a healthy and empowering lifestyle, feeling successful and pursuing your dreams & goals! Thank you for allowing us to be a part of your amazing journey!

Welcome to

THRIVE

A Resilience Program for Teens

Summary

Thrive is an evidence and trauma informed interactive course designed to empower teens with knowledge and tools to thrive in today's culture. Thrive addresses the challenges facing teens with a focus on the risk and protective factors that promote positive choices and healthy behaviors.

The *Thrive* model is intentional about creating a positive atmosphere that addresses unhealthy behavior while encouraging the participants to see their value, focus on solutions and internalize healthy lifestyles.

Thrive topics include Stress and the Body, Identifying Emotions, Sense of Purpose and Strength of Character, Risk and Choices, Influence, Optimism, C.A.R (Cope-Assess-Respond) Method, Taking Active Responsibility and Resistance Training.

Thrive incorporates interactive discussion, worksheets, role-play, video and testimonies.

Acknowledgments

We want to extend a heartfelt thank you to the many individuals who have made an impact in our lives and contributed to this content; family, friends, teachers, coaches, pastors, foster parents and families, co-workers, etc.

An extended thank you goes out to the following individuals and organizations who helped pilot the material and put it in curriculum format:

Willis Jr High School students and staff – Chandler Unified School District, Chandler, AZ

ICAN – "Positive Programs for Youth", Chandler, AZ

CCYSA (Chandler Coalition on Youth Substance Abuse) and the Chandler/Gilbert Substance Misuse and Treatment Task Force

Arizona National Guard Counter Drug Task Force

Pima County Community Prevention Coalition & Executive Director Amy Bass

To Obtain Materials and Train the Trainer Workshop Please Contact:

huntingtonted@gmail.com or empoweringbreakthrough.com

Published by: Empowering Breakthrough

PO Box 272847 | Fort Collins, CO 80527

Table of Contents

References

2020 Arizona Youth Survey (Arizona Criminal Justice Commission)

Monitoring the Future 2018 Survey

SAMHSA - Substance Abuse and Mental Health Services Administration

Arizona Trauma Institute

The Arizona ACEs Consortium

National Institute on Drug Abuse

The Arizona Adverse Childhood Experiences Consortium

ICAN – "Positive Programs for Youth" Chandler, AZ

7 C's of Resilience – Dr. Ginsburg

Dr. Scott Nelson - (PhD) Licensed Psychologist and Certified School Psychologist

Resilience

Resilience is described as a human ability to recover quickly from disruptive change or misfortune without being overwhelmed or acting in dysfunctional or harmful ways. To be resilient includes the ability to cope with the stresses of everyday life and to spring back after suffering through difficult and stressful times.

Positive Mental Health

A state of well-being where individuals can realize their own potential, work productively, cope with the normal stresses of life and be a positive member of the community.

Being mentally healthy is predominantly about the presence of positive characteristics such as a feeling of purpose, contentment, maintaining fulfilling relationships and participating in life to the fullest.

Student Introduction

You are extraordinary. You have your own uniqueness, including amazing gifts and talents that are meant to not only empower you but to benefit others and the world around you. You have within you the ability and power to not only overcome the challenges you face but to transform your challenges into opportunities to grow and fulfill your dreams and goals. We all face unique circumstances in life; however, we are not defined by or limited to them.

You have the ability and power to not only survive your challenges and circumstances but to THRIVE because of them. Resilience and positive mental health skills and attitudes are vital for being able to thrive in today's culture. The great thing is, they can be learned and strengthened!

Stress and challenging events can cause us to experience a flood of powerful negative thoughts, feelings and emotions, which may include anger, anxiety and depression. All of which are normal feelings felt by every human. We can learn and improve our skills to cope and deal with them in a healthy and productive way.

We want to see you THRIVE and experience a healthy and empowering lifestyle, feeling successful and pursuing your dreams and goals! Thank you for allowing us to be a part of your amazing journey!

LESSON 1

Stress/Body

Thrive

Stress and the Body

Lesson 1

LESSON CONCEPT

Resilience is being able to "deal with" and "bounce back" from hard and challenging things in life. We all have challenges. How we "cope" and "deal with" our challenges are important. We cannot always control things that happen to us, but we can learn ways to help us, not just "get through" them, but learn from them and even become stronger. The great news is, we can learn and develop skills to help us overcome challenges, make positive choices and achieve our goals and dreams.

Stress is a part of life. Stress can have good and bad effects on our emotions and bodies. Understanding what causes stress and how it affects our bodies is important. Stress can cause us to act in ways that cause more problems. Most of the time, our reactions to stress are not healthy, and we can do or say things that can be negative. Learning to identify the effects of stress on our emotions and bodies helps us recognize when it is happening and change the way we act and "deal with" stress.

Mindfulness is a technique that is being taught at many schools. Mindfulness means maintaining a moment by moment awareness of our thoughts, feelings, bodily sensations and what is happening around us. We tend to be on autopilot or focused on a past event, or thinking of a future event and not slow down and concentrate on the present and ultimately relax. Using tools that help us be more **Mindful** helps us to reduce our stress, remain calmer and act in positive ways.

LEARNING OBJECTIVES

The objective of this lesson is for each student to understand the affects of stress

1. Explain the definition of resilience

2. Describe stressors in life

3. Explain how stress affects a person physically and emotionally

4. Explain the difference between negative and positive stress

5. Predict when to use the 4 step breathing technique

Activity 1: "Your Stressors" - Fill in the Box Below

WHAT ARE SOME CAUSES OF STRESS?

Activity 2: Stress/Fight or Flight

STRESS	FIGHT OR FLIGHT
• Stress is our body's way of responding to an event or experience. It can be through any of our 5 senses (sight, hearing, touch, taste, smell).	· Fight or flight releases adrenaline and cortisol into our bodies.
· It can be caused by both good and bad experiences.	· It makes our heart beat faster.
· Stress can be both positive and negative.	· We go from using the thinking part of the brain to the response part of our brain.
· We react to stress through thoughts, feelings and emotions.	· Causes the brain to seek quick responses and choices.
	· It makes us more reactive.

Activity 3: "Stress Mode" and "Chill Mode"

STRESS MODE
DISRUPTIVE STATE
Stressed, Anxious, Raging, Amped...

CHILL MODE
CONTROLLED STATE
Relaxed, Taking it easy, Calm...

Can you tell when you are in "STRESS" mode? _____

Can you tell when you are in "CHILL" mode? _____

What are some of the feelings and emotions you have during "STRESS" mode?

_____
_____
_____
_____

What are some of the feelings and emotions you have during "CHILL" mode?

_____
_____
_____
_____

How do you feel physically when you are in "STRESS" mode?

_____
_____
_____
_____

How do you feel physically when you are in "CHILL" mode?

_____
_____
_____
_____

Activity 4: "Responding vs Reacting"

RESPONDING VS REACTING

1) Create a "pause"

2) Four count breathing

3) Focus on relaxing

4) Think of how you want to respond

Activity 5: Three Minute Relaxation Session

- Sit with your feet flat on the floor and arms resting comfortably
- Close your eyes if you feel comfortable doing so
- Focus on relaxing your entire body - from your head to your feet
- Breath using the four-count method - during the entire session - when you exhale, focus on relaxing deeper each time
- If your mind and thoughts start to wander - don't worry - just concentrate on counting your breaths

LESSON 2

Identifying Emotions

Thrive

Identifying Emotions

Lesson 2

LESSON CONCEPTS

We all have emotions. They are normal, and everybody has them. Strong emotions can cause us to feel stress, anxiety and even depression type feelings. Strong emotions can also make us act out and behave in harmful and unhealthy ways (yelling, fighting, hurting ourselves, using substances, etc.). Holding back our emotions is not healthy for us. Learning to recognize, deal and cope with (or regulate) our emotions is our goal.

This lesson will provide different ways to help us deal and cope with our emotions. The more we learn to identify our emotions (anger, frustration, disappointment, etc.) and what causes (or triggers) us to have strong emotions, the easier it is to deal with them in positive ways.

Having people in our lives that we can trust and turn to for support when we are experiencing strong emotions and going through difficult times is extremely important. We call this having a "Support System". We all need others for support. Asking for help and support is a very mature thing to do. Support comes from a variety of areas and people: family, friends and others (professionals, teachers, coaches, faith-based, etc.). It is important to identify several positive role models provide that positive support.

LEARNING OBJECTIVES

The objective of this lesson is for each student to understand emotions and healthy coping skills

1. Describe basic emotions
2. Explain common triggers
3. Explain basic coping skills
4. Explain their support system

Activity 1: Fill in the Blank

1. Emotions are a normal part of life
2. Emotions can be positive or negative
3. Emotions first start to RISE—then calm down
4. Emotions can be _____ (coped with)

Activity 2: Identifying Common Emotions

Activity 3: Identifying Triggers

What can "Trigger" strong emotions for you?	Name the emotions	How do you normally respond?	How do you Want to Respond?
1.			
2.			
3.			
4.			
5.			

Activity 4: Coping Skills

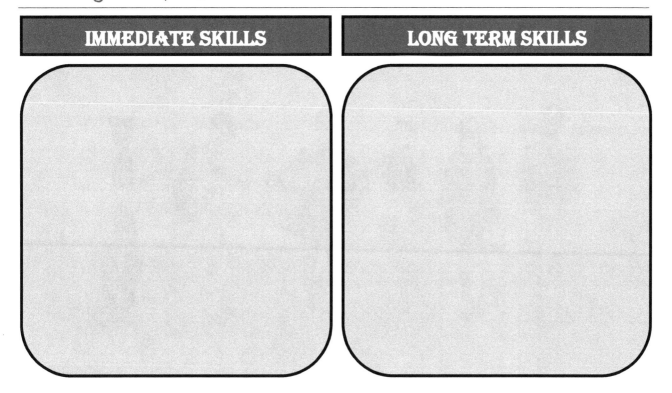

IMMEDIATE SKILLS	LONG TERM SKILLS

Activity 5: Support Systems

FAMILY	FRIENDS	PROFESSIONALS AND OTHERS

LESSON 3

Sense of Purpose -
Strength of Character

Thrive

Student Workbook

LESSON 3

LESSON CONCEPTS

"When you know who you are, you know what you can do!"

You are extraordinary and unique. Each one of you have your own goals to reach, talents to use and explore, passions that motivate you and dreams & purposes to accomplish. You all have your own unique genetic make-up, families, traditions and history. You are essential and you have important roles that you play in other people's lives. Knowing these things about ourselves is called having a "Sense of Purpose."

Our character, core values and morals are the personal traits that we believe are important and how we want people to describe us. Values, such as being loyal, non-judgmental, compassionate, courageous, honest, funny and having faith, are all examples of "Strength of Character." What adds to our strength is that they are our very own and no one and nothing can take them away from us.

"Sense of Purpose" and "Strength of Character" combined helps us define our identity or, "who we are." This is extremely important when it comes to getting through hard & challenging times, and for making our choices.

If we focus on our "Sense of Purpose" and "Strength of Character" when we are going through tough times we have a better chance of finding the hope and courage to believe we can overcome the challenge and not only survive, but, **Thrive** and find something good can come out of it.

LEARNING OBJECTIVES

The objective of this lesson is for each student to understand good character and healthy motivation

1. Explain sense of purpose and strength of character

2. Explain the importance of having goals

3. Describe personal morals and character values

4. Explain positive impact

Activity 1: Interests/Activities Chart

WHAT DO YOU ENJOY DOING MOST?	WHAT DO OTHERS SAY YOU'RE GOOD AT?	WHAT ARE YOU IN-VOLVED WITH NOW?

Lesson 3   Sense of Purpose - Strength of Character

Activity 2: Goals

LIST 3 GOALS YOU WANT TO ACHIEVE THIS YEAR

LIST 3 GOALS TO ACHIEVE BY THE TIME YOU GRADUATE HIGH SCHOOL

LIST 3 GOALS TO ACHIEVE WITHIN THE NEXT 10 YEARS

Activity 3: Who Are You!

YOU	FAMILY	CLOSE FRIENDS

YOUR RELATIONSHIP TITLES (SISTER, BROTHER, FRIEND) CULTURE - HERITAGE	WHAT YOU DO (ATHLETE, STUDENT, GAMER, SINGER)	HOW DO YOU IMPACT OTHERS IN A POSITIVE WAY

LESSON 4

Influence

Thrive

Influence

Lesson 4

LESSON CONCEPTS

What we believe and how we make our choices is based on what we allow to influence us. Influences can come from people or different types of sources (social media, music, trends, our faith, or beliefs, etc.) and can be both positive and negative. Peer pressure has been identified as a major influencer for teens. An everyday fear teens face is worrying about what others think and being judged. This influences their choices and how they view themselves. We all must decide what we allow to influence us and what we choose to be healthy and important. The better we can define our morals/character, goals and sense of purpose, the easier it is to recognize negative influences and avoid or not get involved with them.

Positive activities with other positive peers are a major factor in avoiding unhealthy behavior. It is human nature to act and think like the people and sources we spend time with and choose to be involved with. The simple truth is who we hang out with and what sources we focus on will have a major impact on our lives and our futures. We all must choose!

Young adults today have a great opportunity to be a positive influence. We all have a positive or negative effect on others. Being a positive influence for others makes a positive impact on their lives.

LEARNING OBJECTIVES

The objective of this lesson is for each student to understand how influence effects behavior

1. Describe the impact influence has on making choices

2. Identify people and sources that can influence you

3. Describe how influences can be positive for you

4. Describe how negative influences can affect you

5. Describe how you influence others

Activity 1: Influences Chart

TYPES OF PEOPLE	WHY/HOW DO THEY INFLUENCE YOU	POSITIVE/NEGATIVE

TYPES OF SOURCES	WHY/HOW DO THEY INFLUENCE YOU	POSITIVE/NEGATIVE

Activity 2: Influencer Chart

How do you influence others?

YOUR ACTIONS (WHAT DO YOU SAY OR DO THAT INFLUENCES OTHERS IN A POSITIVE WAY?)

LESSON 5

Risks and Choices

Thrive

Risks & Choices

Lesson 5

LESSON CONCEPTS

We must make choices and take risks every day. This is a natural process of how we learn by our experiences. Each choice we make and the risk we take comes with consequences. The consequences can be both positive and negative. Sometimes even making choices and taking risks to "do the right thing" can feel uncomfortable at the time, but, allows us to achieve our goals in the future.

It takes courage to say "yes" to the positive or healthy risks and choices and courage to say "no" to the negative ones.

The fear of being judged by what others think and the fear of failure can have a big effect on the risks we take. We can make decisions in a hurry without thinking of what the consequences can be until later on, or how they can hurt and affect others. It is also normal to take a risk that seems easier or feels good at the time, but, can later cause us a lot of problems.

A "Good" risk is taking a positive risk and getting out of our comfort zone to make positive choices, even if it is difficult or uncomfortable. This choice includes risking being judged by others, maybe failing, or not doing well at something. This means taking risks to pursue positive plans and goals. If we do not take positive risks (trying out for a sports team or meeting new people), we will not experience the goal. This also helps us see possible failure as an opportunity to learn and grow.

A "Low" risk is making choices that are not likely to result in failure, harm, or injury and are unlikely to be connected with danger or problems.

A "Medium" risks is making choices that will most likely result in some sort of pain, discomfort, or negative consequence. Usually, they are risks that are made at the moment and feel good at the time but are followed with negative results (staying up late, not doing homework or ditching class). As we get older, it is natural to want more freedom. We can take risks to push boundaries and experiment. These risks also allow us to experience negative consequences and learn from them. The message for taking "medium" risks is that it is a natural part of growing up, but it is important to learn from them and make changes to avoid them in the future.

A "High" risk represents life-changing choices and risks that will affect us and others profoundly (misusing drugs, illegal activity, unprotected sex and distracted driving). These result in consequences that cannot be reversed and create challenges that make it difficult for us to accomplish our goals.

LEARNING OBJECTIVES

The objective of this lesson is for each student to understand risk & consequences

1. Describe why making positive choices requires courage.

2. Explain the positive results that can come from good risks.

3. Explain the consequences that can result from Low, Medium and High Risk choices.

Activity 1: Good Risks

GOOD RISK

Activity 2: Risks Chart

LOW RISK	MEDIUM RISK	HIGH RISK

ACTIVITY 3: RISK ASSESSMENT CHART

CHOICE (GOOD RISK)	CONSEQUENCES ON PERSON	CONSEQUENCES ON OTHERS

CHOICE (LOW RISK)	CONSEQUENCES ON PERSON	CONSEQUENCES ON OTHERS

CHOICE (MEDIUM RISK)	CONSEQUENCES ON PERSON	CONSEQUENCES ON OTHERS

CHOICE (HIGH RISK)	CONSEQUENCES ON PERSON	CONSEQUENCES ON OTHERS

LESSON 6

Optimism

Thrive

Optimism

Lesson 6

LESSON CONCEPTS

Being positive or optimistic is extremely important to being resilient. Optimistic thinking gives us the ability to not only overcome difficult challenges but allows us to turn a situation that would and could cause us a lot of problems into something good.

Having challenges is a real and natural part of life. We cannot avoid challenges. How we respond to adversity and challenging situations is extremely important.

Re-directing negative thoughts to positive, optimistic ones: Our natural tendencies are to lean towards negative thoughts and attitudes. Although this is often the easier way and may offer some brief relief, it usually comes with a cost and negative effects. Assessing our thoughts and attitudes for the facts, positive influence and comparing them against our character beliefs helps us identify the negatives. This assessment allows us to determine how to move forward and redirect them.

Optimistic vs. negative thought concepts: The concepts help to identify and give relatable examples to optimistic/negative thought patterns and what these look like in real-life experiences. We will go over positive and negative thought concepts and how to identify optimistic and negative thinking. We will also discuss how to redirect a Pessimistic thought into an Optimistic thought.

.

LESSON OBJECTIVES

The objective of this lesson is for each student to understand the benefits of an optimistic attitude and thinking and how to change a pessimistic attitude

1. The student will identify the characteristics of Pessimism and Optimism

2. The student will understand that they have control of their attitude and how they choose to view a situation

3. The student will identify Pessimistic and Optimistic thought patterns

4. The student will practice changing a Pessimistic thought or attitude to an

Optimistic thought or attitude

Characteristics

- Are thought out over a longer period of time
- Gives us more control
- Help manage the strong immediate emotions
- Find solutions/answers
- Help us do the right thing
- Based more on the facts rather than immediate emotions

Characteristics

- Reactionary/automatic
- Increase negative emotions
- Based on immediate emotions rather than facts
- Focused on past negative experiences

Activity 1: Change and Control

THINGS WE **CANNOT** CHANGE	THINGS WE **CAN** CHANGE

Examples of Pessimistic & Optimistic Thinking concepts

FEARFUL / DOUBTFUL

- Afraid of being judged or embarrassed
- Afraid of failure or a negative outcome
- Doubt their ability
- Question if something is possible

HOPEFUL / DETERMINED

- Accepts the things that they can't control or can't be changed
- Confident in themselves—believes they can if they try
- Focuses on their goals
- Focuses on what they can control

DISCOURAGED

- Feeling overwhelmed.
- Lack of confidence
- Looks for excuses
- Wants to give up or stop trying to find a solution

EMPOWERED

- Realizes challenges, and setbacks happen to everyone and they are an opportunity to get improve / learn.
- Believes they have strength/courage and values within them to overcome their challenge
- Stays calm, takes responsibility and focuses on finding a solution

ANGRY / RESENTFUL

- Feels they are being controlled
- Focuses on getting revenge
- Feels jealous and envious of others
- Focusing on the negative or bad in a situation or person.

GRATEFUL

- Focuses on things they are grateful for.
- Knows there are others that are facing challenges as well
- Tries to be forgiving

Activity 2: Re-Directing Negative Thoughts

Pessimistic—to—Optimistic

SCENARIO SITUATIONS	PESSIMISTIC THOUGHT REACTION	OPTIMISTIC THOUGHT RE-DIRECTION
1. You receive negative or judgmental responses to a social media post.		
2. School policy does not allow you to wear your favorite clothes.		
3. Your teams loses it's 4th competition in a row.		
4. You want to try out for a part in a play and find out that 20 other people are trying out for the same part too.		
5. You find out that your best friend will be moving out of state.		
6.		
7.		
8.		

LESSON 7

Taking Active Responsibility

Thrive

Taking Active Responsibility

LESSON 7

LESSON CONCEPTS

Learning to take responsibility for our actions is one of the most important things we can do in life. It doesn't always feel good at the time, but it really helps us mature and become stronger. It means doing things like admitting when we are wrong, didn't make the best choice, or not blaming someone and something else. It means taking responsibility for our own actions, which teaches us how to become mentally and emotionally healthy, independent adults.

Our natural tendency is to shift the blame and justify our actions by taking the easy way and have someone else clean up the mess that our actions and choices created. Taking responsibility for our actions is very empowering. It allows us to grow in leaps and bounds & creates opportunities and more freedom. Another great thing, when we take responsibility for our actions, other people respect us.

Taking charge of our lives requires us to take action steps. We call this being pro-active. We will create a proactive plan that will help us avoid common challenges like procrastinating and being inconsistent. We will focus on ways to be proactive and consistent. We will list ways to be active by getting involved with the things we like to do and connecting with others who are also doing positive, fun and healthy activities.

LEARNING OBJECTIVES

The objective of this lesson is for each student to understand responsibility

1. In your own words, explain accountability

2. Create action steps to be proactive and strengthen accountability

3. Identify other positive people being positive and proactive and how you can connect with them.

Activity 1: Action/Accountability Chart

EXAMPLES OF BLAME SHIFTING/JUSTIFYING BE-HAVIOR	ACTION, ACCOUNTABILITY, EMPOWERMENT STEP (WHAT CAN BE DONE TO TAKE RESPONSIBILITY)	POSITIVE RESULTS FOR ACCEPTING RESPONSIBILITY
1.<u>Not wanting to be wrong or accept responsibility</u> (List an example):	1.	1.
2. <u>Not wanting to accept consequences for our be-havior</u> (List an example):	2.	2.
3. <u>Wanting to take the easy way out instead of doing what's right</u> (List an example):	3.	3.

Activity 2: Proactive Plan

Avoid Procrastinating

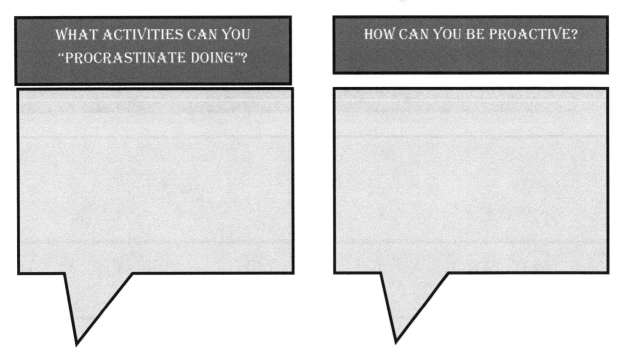

Focus on Consistency

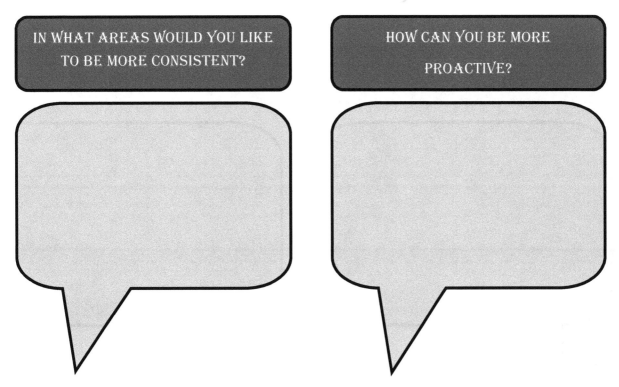

Lesson 7   Taking Active Responsibility

Ways to Help Empower Others

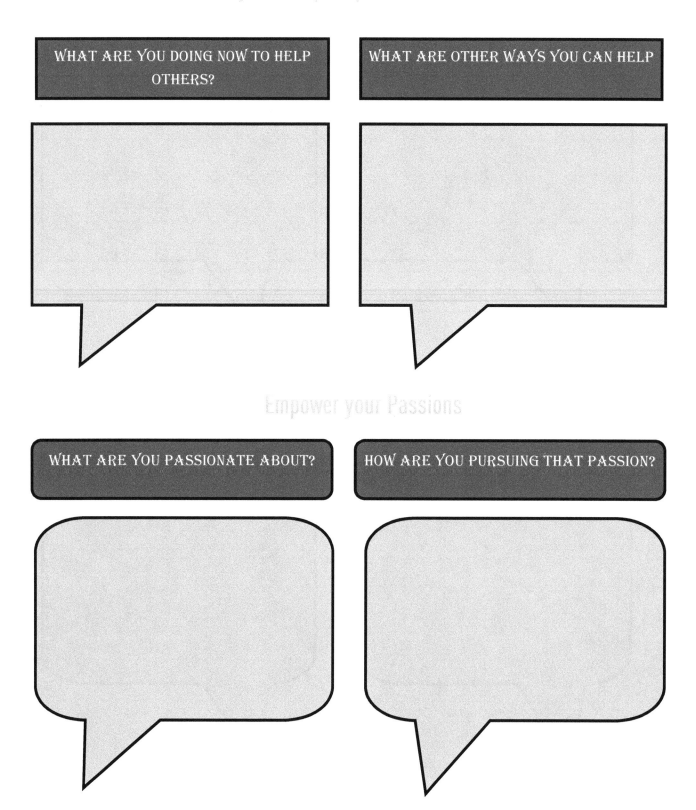

WHAT ARE YOU DOING NOW TO HELP OTHERS?

WHAT ARE OTHER WAYS YOU CAN HELP

Empower your Passions

WHAT ARE YOU PASSIONATE ABOUT?

HOW ARE YOU PURSUING THAT PASSION?

Activity #3: Connect with Positive and Proactive People

WHO ARE THE PEOPLE YOU KNOW DOING POSITIVE AND PROACTIVE THINGS?	HOW ARE YOU CONNECTING WITH THEM?	WHAT ELSE CAN I DO TO CONNECT WITH POSITIVE AND PROACTIVE PEOPLE?

Positive Connections

LESSON 8

Substance Misuse
and
Just the Facts...You Decide

Thrive

Substance Misuse &Just the facts...You Decide

Lesson 8

LESSON CONCEPTS

This lesson will address the facts surrounding the dangers and risks of teen substance use and misuse. We understand you are mature individuals who have your own life experiences. We really respect that you are all individuals and have the freedom and power to make up your own minds and make your own choices. We all have our personal unique life stories and experiences. We hope to use this lesson to share some important facts about substances and our knowledge from our own experience as well.

In lesson 5, we learned about Risks and Choices. We used "High Risks" as the ones that can cause life-changing consequences and have a devastating effect on others. Drugs and substance misuse are "High Risks." You may know a family member, friend or a well-known celebrity or media figure that struggles with addiction or even died from an accidental overdose. No one becomes addicted to a substance overnight. It usually happens in stages that are not even noticeable to the person that it is happening. Addiction affects the brain, and that is why it is classified as a disease. Once a person's brain becomes either dependent or addicted to a substance, that person usually needs professional help to become sober again.

The nicotine content in most vape and e-cigarette products is also addicting. Most teens who struggle with vaping and do want to slow down or stop, are frustrated with the facts that they crave it and have a very hard time quitting. Knowing the facts about addiction and the brain gives us the best chance to seek the right support and take control, instead of being controlled by the substance.

LEARNING OBJECTIVES

The objective of this lesson is for you to...

1. Learn the common substances being misused today

2. Learn facts surrounding the dangers and negative effects of substance misuse

3. Learn common reasons why teens engage in substance misuse

4. Learn the 5 stages of addiction

Activity 1: Facts — Common Substances Used by Teens

> 1. Alcohol, Marijuana and _____.
> 2. The most popular way to consume Marijuana and tobacco is through: _____ and E-Cigarette Products.

Activity 2: Facts — Effects of Substance Use for Teens

> 1. The average age Teens start to experiment/use is _____ years old. (Nationwide)
> 2. Teens who use substances before age 15 are 5 times more likely to develop a dependence or _____.

Activity 3: Facts — Common Reasons for Teen Substance Use

> 1. For _____, are bored, want to experiment.
> 2. Do not realize the dangers of substance use.
> 3. Family Conflict or other stressors.

Activity 4: Facts — 5 Stages of Addiction

> 1. First Use
> 2. _____ Use
> 3. Tolerance
> 4. Dependence
> 5. Addiction

Activity 5: Facts — Real Testimony from a Real Teen

LIST THE SUBSTANCES USED BY THE SPEAKER	LIST SOME OF THE UN-HEALTHY OR NEGATIVE BEHAVIORS THE SPEAKER MENTIONED.
LIST THE STAGES OF ADDIC-TION THE SPEAKER EXPERIENCED	LIST SOME OF THE POSITIVE THINGS THE SPEAKER IS DOING NOW THAT HE/SHE GOT HELP AND IS IN RECOVERY

LESSON 9

Resistance Skills

Thrive

Resistance Skills

Lesson 9

LESSON CONCEPTS

So you have decided to take a positive risk to say "No" to something you do not want to do or get involved with. It can be hard standing up to peer pressure or other influences.

All situations are not the same. Temptations and pressure can come from a lot of different places like social media, peers, a stranger, a friend or even family. We can feel really strong about saying "No" sometimes and other times need a good excuse to use to avoid trouble. We may also have to resist a friend or family member and not want to hurt their feelings.

Resistance skills give us examples and tools to help us resist the temptations and influences, get out of tough situations and even be a good example for others. Sometimes, for the people we care about, we can help them resist by redirecting them to something else.

In this lesson, we will go over a variety of ways to say "No" and resist. We will go over some examples of how to make positive excuses to get out of tough situations and also how to redirect the person or group to do something better instead. This lesson will also let you practice by role-playing and let you share some of the excellent skills that you know and have used.

LEARNING OBJECTIVES

The objective of this lesson is for you to understand how to avoid risky behaviors and negative thoughts

1. You will learn a 5-step method for resisting peer pressure and temptations to avoid getting involved in risky behaviors

2. You will learn examples of the Resistance Strategy Statements

3. You will practice applying the resistance skills through scenarios

Skill: 5 Step Method for Resistance

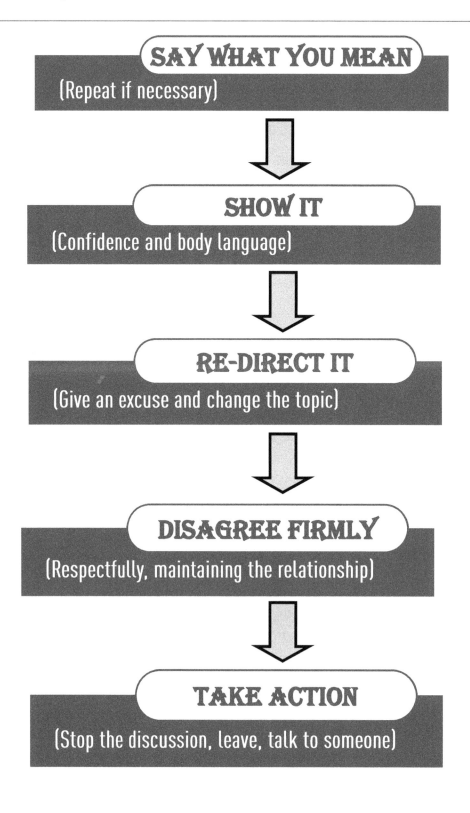

SAY WHAT YOU MEAN
(Repeat if necessary)

SHOW IT
(Confidence and body language)

RE-DIRECT IT
(Give an excuse and change the topic)

DISAGREE FIRMLY
(Respectfully, maintaining the relationship)

TAKE ACTION
(Stop the discussion, leave, talk to someone)

Activity 1: Examples of Strategies

REMOVAL

"Thanks for inviting me, but I can't, my parents are coming to pick me up, and I have to go."

(Your "REMOVAL" Statement)

IT IS NOT NORMAL

" I know you think everyone's doing it, but I have a lot of friends who don't."

"My basketball team made an agreement with each other to stay away from_____."

(Your "IT IS NOT NORMAL" Statement)

CONSEQUENCES

"Dad would lose it if he found out we had a party."

-

"It will affect our performance on the basketball court and ruin our shot at state."

(Your "CONSEQUENCES" Statement)

Tips to promote Resilience and Positive Mental Health

Get regular exercise

Eat regular meals

Avoid using excessive caffeine *(coffee, tea, energy drinks, soft drinks, etc.)*

Avoid illegal drugs, alcohol, and tobacco

Learn relaxation techniques *(e.g., mindfulness skills, deep breathing, progressive muscle relaxation, meditation)*

Develop assertiveness skills *(e.g., how politely but firmly say "no," or state one's feelings)*

Rehearse and practice responses to stressful situations

Break down large tasks into smaller, more attainable tasks

Learn to recognize and reduce negative self-talk; challenge negative thoughts about oneself with alternative neutral or positive thoughts

Avoid demanding perfection from oneself or others; instead, learn to feel good about doing a competent or "good enough" job.

Take a break from stressful activities or situations. Engage in a hobby, listen to music, or spend time with a pet.

Build a network of friends who can help one to cope in positive ways

(Source: American Academy of Child & Adolescent Psychiatry)

CPSIA information can be obtained
at www.ICGtesting.com
Printed in the USA
BVHW010816311021
620155BV00008B/17